Lady Boss Blueprint

How to Reframe your Business to Create the Life of Your Dreams

BY

COURTNEY WRIGHT

Ordering Information: Quantity sales. Special discounts are available on quantity purchases by corporations, associations and others. Orders by U.S. trade bookstores and wholesalers.

www.DreamStartersPublishing.com

Table of Contents

Foreword

I want to take a minute to tell you why I wrote this book and thank the people who made it a reality. Back about a year ago as I was trying to grow my podcast someone mentioned that I'd be a much more formidable guest on others podcast if I had a book published.

You're about to see that everything in my life has been very planned out and very mapped out multiple years in advance and there was definitely no mention of a book on any of my goals sheets previously. You're also about to find out that I am someone who doesn't overthink opportunities. I try them and sometimes they work and sometimes they don't. I'm not particularly afraid of failure. I'm much more afraid of not learning and progressing forward.

I thought let me take a stab at writing this book Because I had a burning desire and a realization after my dad passed that life is so short and I know that sounds very funny coming from someone that is in the late 50s but when you work as hard as I do to feel well, it just didn't dawn on me until a few years ago that the ride we have on this planet we are so lucky for every day and we don't know what we are going to get and for how long.

I wanted to take this opportunity before it wasn't available to me to thank all the people that have helped me on my entrepreneurial journey because it's been just that, it's been a journey. It's had a lot of ups and downs and it's also been something that I'm very proud of. Thank you for buying this book and thank you for being part of my thank you note.

I want to particularly call out two people. Alex Hunt on my team at Gemini and Frank Fontana of Fontana Creative, they have bore the heavy lifting of the podcast, and day and day out, have seen the challenges of doing it, while running my companies, their unwavering commitment to make things look the way we wanted online and to make things happen is something I appreciate beyond measure.

I also want to thank my girl squad who keeps encouraging me to move forward even though at this point in the juncture, I'm wondering why I ever had this idea. My Mom, my true north and biggest inspiration engrained in me that I can do anything, and I am eternally grateful for her and her selfless love for me. Fear is the only thing speaking as I sum this up, and I really don't want to publish this, simply because of fear.

I have also learned and come to grips with the fact that fear is something we have to push through in order to get better, so thank you for indulging me on my path to getting better because for me that is what it's all about. Cheers!!!!

Courtney Wright

Introduction

In what ways can you change the world?

"I like to say it's an attitude of not just thinking outside the box, but not even seeing the box."

Safra. A. Catz

Many believe that only men can run the world, armed forces and corporations and I say, that's bullshit. True, throughout history men have predominantly held positions of power, leadership and have accomplished great things. Times have changed, and now there is another powerful force that lurks behind the scenes that many don't and won't see coming. The birth of women entrepreneurs, businesswomen, CEOs, leaders and innovators are on the rise. In 1972, there were only 400,000 businesses owned by women, by 2020, 42% of businesses were owned by women. These are the women who were born to be a "Lady Boss". They know what they want out of life, take no crap and work not just as hard, but many times harder than their male counterparts just to gain the same respect.

These entrepreneurs can be solopreneurs, those with side hustles starting out, the stay-at-home mom starting a business on the side and anyone that wants to work for themselves in some capacity. Stepping into a leadership, entrepreneurial or CEO role as a woman can be challenging for those who are not equipped and focused on their mission. Claiming your seat at the table or even bringing your own seat requires you to be assertive, know what you want, have confidence in who you are, trust your skills, and have the ability to persevere.

In modern society, women are wearing multiple hats while juggling their careers, marriages, children, friends and life. Let's be honest, in many homes the woman is believed to be the one that tends to cook, clean and nurture her family. Trying to rise to the top professionally in a male dominated work culture is an added battle that most don't know how to fight. Many women put their dreams and aspirations on the backburner or are afraid of trying to achieve their goals. Some women may already be entrepreneurs and think, "Oh crap, I've got this business, I don't know what to do and don't have the money to do what I want." Many do not have the resources, time, or money to be able to cut the system short. Also, it's not as if their male counterparts, colleagues and bosses are helping them climb the ladder. Some may help, but they are the exception.

What if I told you that you can have it all? The fulfilling career, business, the leadership position and you can make it a reality.

I'm Courtney Wright, entrepreneur, CEO, strategist and owner **of Lady Boss Podcast with Courtney Wright.** I am a visionary in the business world who, with creative innovation, has been able to translate my client's ideas into accomplishments and connect the dots. Growing up, I have always believed that I could be anyone I wanted to be. I knew that I was not going to let anything stop me from having my cake and eating it too. Since the age of seven, the sales process has always fascinated me. At that time, I was in the Girl Scouts and was determined to sell more Girl Scout cookies than any other girl in my troop, which I did.

A challenge has never deterred me. I have grown up witnessing entrepreneurs in a business family and would consider myself a smart, educated woman and was a member of a business networking and peer-to-peer group (Vistage) much of my adult life. Despite my advantages, I still made a multitude of mistakes that were expensive and time consuming. My passion and desire are to be a beacon of light to other women entrepreneurs, leaders and CEOs. I want to help women get "further, faster". If I can prevent a woman from making some of the mistakes I have made and provide guidance to help light the way, then my job is done.

COURTNEY WRIGHT

Early in my career, I set a goal to build and sell a successful business within ten years. To most people, that sounds crazy and rightfully so, it sounded crazy to me too. CDW Merchants was a company I started in 2006 and sold in 2012. I set my vision, went to work and since then have not only accomplished building and selling a business, but currently own multiple businesses: Gemini Builds It, Showcase Acrylics, an E-commerce company as well as my podcast, Lady Boss with Courtney Wright.

Growing up, my father would always tell me that I could be anything I wanted to be. I was also naive because at the age of twenty-two, after getting into the real world, I discovered that it was a bunch of bull. I found out there were not many other women working with me in management or corporate positions. It was a boy's club and most of the time, I was alone as the only woman. I thought to myself, "What was my dad talking about?" One dude gave me the "Heisman" then another dude would give me the "Heisman." It's like they would all run in another direction whenever I came around and soon it reinforced the belief I always had regarding myself, that I would be able get to wherever I chose. I want women to learn to drown out all the noise, forget the fact that it is a boy's club and let's get further, faster. Despite all the obstacles thrown our way, we can *still* be anything we want to be.

Join me through my journey in business and entrepreneurship as I share my life stories and lessons along the way. Learn ways to not only build your business, but also scale your business to where you want it to be. Learn how to be one of the most valuable players in this male dominated game of business. Gain key insights on how to use your creativity and innovation to carve out a place for yourself in the market. If you are seeking ways to awaken the potential that is brewing inside of you and are ready to step up to the plate as a “Lady Boss”, let’s dive in!

Takeaways

- What inspires you to want a leadership role or to become an entrepreneur? Ask yourself five times to get the real answer.
- How do you prioritize your work life balance while pursuing your passion?
- Are you ready to put the knowledge from this book to use?

Chapter 1

Dad- Money Creates Freedom

"You don't find happiness, you create happiness. You don't find success, you create success. You don't find joy, you create joy. Stop searching, start creating."

Tim Grover

I grew up in New England to a middle-class family who raised me to like the finer things in life. I traveled, went to a private Quaker girls' school and had great clothes (of course I did, my father and his family were custom clothiers and entrepreneurs). I grew up around all self-made entrepreneurs and this was in the eighties. Currently, you can find many people with wealth but to be around so many businesspeople with money back then was rare (my dad's customers were high flying CEOs). My father was the epitome of a hard worker. He worked his ass off six days a week, only being off on Sundays. He would usually sleep all day Sunday, so if we wanted to spend time with him, we would go to his clothing store and help fold clothes and talk to him. He was a great salesman and provider for our family. We always had everything we needed and wanted. He did it so effortlessly, I thought it was normal to have a beautiful home, designer clothes and nice cars.

Every night we had dinner as a family. My mom was a homemaker and not in the sense of today's homemakers who have cooks and cleaning ladies. My mother did it ALL. She helped us with our homework, made all our meals from scratch, needle pointed, made crafts and decorated our home, which was always beautiful. She was a renaissance mom, not the call-it-in type we see too often today whose big accomplishment is "lunch." The best advice that I received from my mother was "make your family a priority." This was not just empty advice, she practiced what she preached. My parents were the essence of the American Dream. They believed in the value of work and worked harder than anyone I knew, so it was modelled and expected that I'd work hard too. I always embraced that and had big goals.

My mother knew that I had a love for the French language when I began studying it, she wanted to nurture my desire to learn and researched a French family that participated in the Foreign Exchange program. That allowed me the opportunity to travel to France during the year. I had no idea at that time what the expense for me to travel overseas must have cost my family. I had no trust fund and my father sold suits for a living, to think how he busted his ass so we never felt financial stress blows my mind. That tells me that he must have been one hell of a salesman.

I moved far away to attend college, not because I wanted to be away from my family, but because I wanted the experience of living in a big city. I wanted to continue to grow, be exposed to enriching experiences and broaden my perspectives. After all, instead of going to summer camp in the woods of Maine or Cape Cod like my sister did, I was sent off to Paris for the summers to learn and practice my French. I was a foreign exchange student and stayed with a wonderful family and immersed myself in the language, culture and people. Those trips to France showed me that there is a massive world outside of Rhode Island. A world full of different customs, community, food, clothing and experiences. I learned to speak French fluently and was immensely proud of that. French was one of my greatest skills. I had an ear for the language and heck, why not practice it as often as I could?

I left Providence for Paris each summer during high school, and I would never be the same. My parents were not afraid of exposing me to bigger things and opening my eyes to all that was out there in the world. What a GIFT that was. After graduating college, I landed a job in Chicago at Schwarz Paper Company and continued to live there. You don't go backwards. You don't go back home when you have the chance to do what you went to school to study and dreamed of doing. Moving back to Providence and with my parents was not an option.

When I moved into my nicely appointed first apartment, it came with all the adult responsibilities that included paying my rent. One month, I had to pay rent with a check and remember asking my dad what to do with the check register in the back of the checkbook. Up until that point, I had not written a lot of checks in my life. My parents paid for my college and provided the framework for my spending needs. I had a job during college, but my main goal was focusing on my grades. My parents also wanted me to focus on my grades because like most college students, I learned early on in my college years that naivety and alcohol did not make a good combination. That led me to frantically work on improving my grades with what time I had left. Prioritizing my studies was all I could do to keep up with the schoolwork and graduate on time.

Back to the register, after asking my father what to do with the check register, he very rudimentarily answered the question and his answer was, “Courtney, I’ll tell you what I know, if you need more money, make more money.” True, his response did not answer the original question pertaining to the register in the checkbook, however his reply was a statement that would be forever etched into my psyche.

My father was not good with details, but he was an epic big picture thinker. The big picture he wanted me to know is, if you need more money, go make it. Period. No excuses. My father showed me that I needed to keep a “money creation mindset” knowing that it is okay for me to spend and enjoy myself because I can create ways to earn more. I never forgot his advice and it changed the way I viewed money. The concept of making more money sounds so simple, but let me tell you, it can be hard for many. I see more people who are financially caught up and mentally afraid of money than those who are not. Some people feel guilty for having money or feel they do not deserve any. This fear of money limits their success.

I consider those words my father shared with me **words of abundance** and they essentially set me free from all the self-limiting beliefs, poverty mindsets and pressures of not measuring up. I did not have the baggage that so many carry around regarding success and money. I was free to start my career and do all that I wished to accomplish. I was never stuck like a ball tethering to a pole playing the mental game of how much money I should make in my lifetime or questioning if it's okay to earn a lot of money. Instead, I was asking *how* to make money. All those examples were modelled for me growing up and soon it was time for me to show my parents that I listened to them and learned.

My father, Briggs Austin Doherty, passed away at 77 years of age and his lessons and influence still affect my life to this day. Reflecting on his life, I think about him, his impeccable work ethic, love of family and his love for cars. My father loved not just average cars but nice cars, exotic cars and vintage cars. Automobiles were his guilty pleasure. For the most part, he eventually owned every car that he desired, except for one. He had it on his bucket list that he would purchase himself a Bentley and, despite his best efforts, was unable to make that desire become a reality. Although he was not able to check that off his list, my father did own over 100 cars in his lifetime.

He lived his life, and he loved his life. In the end, he had more cars than years and he took care of every single one of them, the years and the cars. What I learned from my father's life is that you could live 150 years in 77. You can get so much fulfillment from your life to last more than two lifetimes. He also showed me that if I want to do something, I need to do it NOW. No sense in waiting around for what can be done today. Time waits for no one, and no man can control the inevitable phenomena of time.

My husband Larry's family has a different mindset regarding money than the mindset with which I was raised. We had similar upbringings in the fact that both of our fathers were the breadwinners and our mother's stayed at home and cared for the family. His parents were two decades older than my parents, were self-made people, hard workers and lived during the Great Depression. During that time, necessities were scarce and there was not enough food to feed everyone. They believed in saving every dollar earned and after hearing about how they lived during those times it is understandable. Larry's family lived in a beautiful home in a country club community where his parents prudently saved their funds, carefully squirreling it away to eventually leave it to their children.

To this day, if I am going to the grocery store, my mother-in-law will stop me and remind me to get the Publix brand cottage cheese. I guess thriftiness is engrained in them. My in-laws would often look at me and my family and say, "You guys are some spenders!" To which, I would reply, "Well, that's just how we do it." My family was the type that enjoyed the finer things in life. We had a nice house, nice cars, nice clothes and nice vacations. I have memories of going to Europe and my dad taking my kids all over and if they wanted some Gucci shoes, my father would take them to buy Gucci shoes.

My father made sure he enjoyed his money even if he did not have savings to pass down to the next generation. Larry's family took fewer vacations and were more careful about the fruits of their labor. There is so much in this world to see, so many things to experience, we must decide whether we are working to live or living to work. They believed in the power of saving and compound interest. Don't get me wrong, saving and investing with compound interest is a means to retirement and wealth, but I want both. I want the ability to save, invest, gain compound interest and still enjoy my life, family and life's pleasures. I do not want money for material things, **but rather for my freedom**.

I like having the freedom to dictate when I can spend time with my family and where to invest my time and resources. This freedom that I have allowed myself means that I can take my friends out for a nice dinner at any restaurant in any city I like. I enjoy having the ability to purchase any type of shoes I desire and have found that it is fun to do after a hard day's work. Money is a measure of the contribution I make to society. I am never nervous about having to make money because my focus is on making a valuable contribution to my community. The money will follow.

After college, my friends and I secured jobs and we all seemed content. My friends were making $75,000 annually, had the house and felt as though they were living comfortably. Nothing is wrong with that salary, $75,000 is a kick ass amount of money to earn, especially back in the nineties. However, I just knew that I wanted more because of what I wanted to do with my life. I dreamed of becoming a 7-figure earner. I set my sights on that goal and began working towards it. Around 1990, I was twenty-three years old and had been working hard for the company I was employed at.

My manager at the time was this hard-core sales guy who somewhat had an air of cockiness with a dash of toxic masculinity sprinkled into his persona. He, like many of the managers I have met, was part of the boy's club and was the type who naturally expected women to be working in positions under him than on the side of him. One day, I decided that I wanted to have a talk with him to discuss the goals for myself within the company. I told him that my goal for the next year was to make a half million, and as soon as he heard that, he choked on the coffee he was sipping allowing some to escape the corner of his mouth and drip down onto his crispy, ironed white shirt.

I'll never forget that moment and how he was so taken aback by my desire to make more sales. It was as if he had never heard an employee set such a lofty goal for themselves before, let alone a woman. Up until that point, I had earned half that, but wanted to raise the bar. I asked him to tell me what I needed to do for my sales to get there. He began this long rant and went on and on about how I was too focused on money, how money was a measure and how I needed to focus on fulfillment instead of money.

I thought to myself that I was thinking of my happiness and that was why I was still there working for him as opposed to going to another company that would pay me more. It was an awkward position to be in when you think about it because I was wanting to learn valuable ways to help me hit my target. He, on the other hand, was basically telling me to be happy where I was.

That situation made me realize that if I were going to reach higher levels, it certainly wasn't going to be easy, and some people wouldn't be willing to help me. I began to learn about value creation and that became my goal. Value creation is the process of creating additional worth or benefit from either your services or your products. I could add value to my services by taking advantage of my innovative way of thinking and my creativity. It was okay if my boss could not make that happen for me when I asked him and it was something that I had to wrestle with at that time, but I knew in my heart that I wouldn't wrestle with it for long. Even though I may have wanted to negotiate my earnings and worth, working as an employee was not going to allow me to do that. I would have to work for myself and create my own value and worth. Simple as that.

At the end of the day, money is a measure of contribution and value. Employers can only pay someone so much despite their best efforts, however, if I became an entrepreneur, there was no limit. Providing value is equally as important as contributing. Knowing that, I had to make sure that whatever business endeavors I wanted to work my way to, contribution and value had to be the driving force.

Motivational speaker and author, Tony Robbins, often speaks about the importance of adding value to others; it is the main principle needed to achieve your own goals and find fulfillment. Value creation is an important aspect of personal and professional development. Along with providing contributions and value, getting rid of any self-limiting beliefs or scarcity mindsets is also necessary. A scarcity mindset is one that holds a belief that there are not enough resources to go around.

A person with this mindset may feel that everything needed for future progress is scarce or running out. Individuals also may display feelings such as guilt, anger or envy. Often when entrepreneurs are first starting out in their business, they hold on to scarcity beliefs. I DEFINITELY DID. Instead of operating from this way of thinking, adopt an abundance mindset instead. A person with an abundance mindset can take the belief of scarcity and flip it, turning it into a positive thought. They see all the opportunities life has to offer and believe there is an endless supply of resources.

I always express gratitude and know that I possess the skills to pay the bills and do whatever needs to be done. Warren Buffet earned 85% of his wealth after the age of 65. Many women will get older and feel like opportunities have passed them by. That is a lie, regardless of where you are in your life and in your career, change is possible. If you want to make more money, put yourself out there and go make more money. Sometimes, it seems like people have a fear of money. I have seen it with my own eyes with my sales team, how a person will talk themselves out of a sale and out of big deals due to them working out of fear. I have never been afraid of making a mistake, nor have I been afraid that I would lose money in business. None of that mattered when it came down to my wanting to take a risk to gain big rewards. Personally, I don't care if stuff breaks, fear of things that I have not done before will not stop me. I try hard to keep going, and learning….

A book that helped further my knowledge of money management and how to think like the rich was *Rich Dad, Poor Dad (Kiyosaki, Letcher, 1997)*. In this book, Robert Kiyosaki discusses how important financial literacy is. He discusses wealth building to gain financial independence through investing in assets such as real estate. This book taught me all the strategies I needed to improve my cash flow and how the rich think about money. I recommend this book to anyone who is seeking to learn more about financial intelligence. The valuable information provided can assist you in business as well as in life.

In conclusion, when thinking about money remember to look at it as a tool that allows you freedom. The freedom it provides can give you autonomy and control over your life, relationships and career. Money is a measure of contribution that you can make to society and your community. If you want to make more money, find ways that you can become more contributable. Understand the importance of value creation and ways that you can increase your individual or business value. Mega value creation occurs when you add a major value. This pertains to your skills or self-confidence and is often a result of you doing something uncomfortable. **Become more uncomfortable because that is where the opportunity lies.** There is more than enough out there to go around. Get out there and get your piece of the pie.

Takeaways

- Reflect on the relationship you have with money.
- Are you using it as a tool?
- Do you control your money, or is money controlling you?

Chapter 2

Invest in Time

"Life-fulfilling work is never about the money- when you feel true passion for something, you instinctively find ways to nurture it."

Eileen Fisher. Fashion designer

When you're constantly working from inside of your business, it can hurt you in the long run. From this position, you are unable to see the big picture to fully understand what moves need to be made. Taking a step back from working in your business to working on your business is sometimes necessary if you have plans to go to the top. Stepping back from the day-to-day operations to focus on your operations allows you to plan strategically on what changes can be made, solve any problems that your business is facing and gives you a picture on how productive and efficient your operation is. This step is crucial for long-term success and to make sure that your business remains competitive and adaptable in the market.

Back in 2006 when I had my first business, my neighbor, Dave, was always watering his lawn in the evenings when I arrived home from work. He would spark up small talk from time to time and from conversations he knew that I owned a business. He would sometimes ask me how my business was going, and my reply was always, “It’s a huge success!” regardless of the state my company was in, it could be going up in flames with shit flying all around and a total disaster, but no one would ever know it. I will tell them it’s awesome every time. Dave was a businessman himself and remarkably successful in his own right. One day, he came to me and told me about a peer-to-peer networking group called Vistage that he thought I should join. He kept telling me I had to do it.

At first, I was hesitant because it was a little expensive to join, with a cost of almost $19,000 annually and I was not thrilled at the fact that they only met once a month. It was hard for me to see the value of joining. I felt as if I didn’t have a day each month to sit and work on my business.

That did not stop Dave and his persistent chipping away at my hesitance every time we spoke. Every day when I got home, he would ask me about my business. Now at that time in my business, I was selling, making the products and acting as the company finance department! It was a busy time for me and by the time I would get home from work in the evenings, I was probably more pessimistic than usual.

One evening, Dave and I were talking, and I guess he could see the exhaustion from the day on my face and urged me one final time to join Vistage. This time I took the bait, applied and was accepted for an interview. Dave was older than me and very successful, so I went for the interview to learn more. There was a chain of command within Vistage, but I paid no mind and decided I wanted to go to the top of the food chain and interview with the head person. The person that is over the largest group in Vistage. My entire life I have always tried to be a small house in a big neighborhood. I always want to learn from the best people, and I feel that I can add tons of value as well, so that is why going to the person who is in charge was my goal.

On your journey, you should find ways to get around the people who try to block you from reaching the person at the top. I asked who the top guy in the organization was and once I found out who he was, I went and interviewed with him. Group 307 was the premier group based out of Chicago and run by Bob Berk (Vistage's “Chair of Chairs”) or the tip of the top.

After speaking with him, he rejected me. He told me that I was too small of a company. I tried explaining to him that I was small at that time because I had just started the business, however I came from a large business background and was in the early stages of getting the business going and could see the flywheel was about to take off. None of that mattered to him because he felt that I had a lot to learn about business and still considered my company not big enough. He told me that I needed to join the smaller business group with Vistage. Reluctantly, I followed his advice, even though I knew that I did not think like a small business owner and did not want a small business. I had big visions for my company and nothing about my visions said “small”.

I joined Vistage in the second year of owning my first business. The small business group that I was in served its purpose for a couple of years. I was then introduced to a man who ended up becoming my advisor and worked with me on the sale of my company and was beneficial to me. After a few years passed, I began to look around and realized that all the members of the group I was in were still thinking small and were still small companies. In my opinion, this was because of their mindsets. They were not doing the work needed to grow.

I knew that I had to get into the large business group because those people were the ones who were hungry, were grinders, took no prisoners and met their goals. I don’t especially like taking no for an answer so when I wanted to upgrade groups, I reapplied and asked for a redo on my interview with the same chairman who originally told me no,

Bob Berk. This time, he accepted me into the large business group and at the end of the meeting said to me, "I'm really sorry for turning you down at first, that might have been the biggest "f---up" of my life. I can't believe I said no to you. What was I thinking?" I thought to myself, "No shit Sherlock."

He included me and I was lucky enough to be in that epic group for many years. At first, I was so scared of him when he finally accepted me into the group. He called it like he saw it and that resonated with me. I always prefer people with a direct tongue and direct feedback. All my mentors have always been direct, while I may appear that I am sensitive, I prefer direct feedback. It comes across clearly, allowing me to soak it in and go forward. I have always been a student of the game and often encourage others to do the same. During our monthly meetings, I made sure to soak up as much information as possible from the other members.

We would often have discussions where Bob would pick at people in our group until the real issue came out. Every month we sat and heard the stories and issues of the CEOs around the table. He would listen to our rants and call bullshit so fast when he could see one of us was camouflaging what the real issue was, most of the time the root of the issue was hiding behind **FEAR**. I gained so much valuable information about being a CEO. One reality that was cemented in my brain was what a CEO's real job entails. They taught me that a CEO's job is to **set the strategy, do the**

biggest deals and hire the best talent. Essentially, it's those three components.

This can be hard to grasp for new business owners who are starting out or buying a business and they have their hands in all the daggers. Sometimes, as a business owner you may not have the infrastructure or resources, however if you stick to those three key components, you will always be successful. I was unaware of many issues that CEOs face. This includes the things that are scary because they have never been done before. Having each other to bounce ideas off was beneficial.

Bob ran a tight ship in that group, but he soon became one of my favorite people. I learned that there was a difference between small business groups and larger business groups. In the smaller business group, the members tended to have a small mindset as well. They just played it safe, and many times did not do their homework thoroughly. The bigger the mindset, the bigger the results. Members in the bigger business groups more than likely had already had their share of failures. They probably had lost money and had broken things in the past. Despite the setbacks, they were not afraid to put themselves out there.

Joining Vistage turned out to be one the best business decisions I have ever made. Those friendships and peers in the room became my "de facto" board of advisors. They were the eighteen people whom I sat with once a month, who had good wishes for me and were not on my payroll. They told me exactly how it was, and I listened exactly as they told it, because each of us wanted everyone around us to succeed.

Despite having never attended business school, the fifteen years I spent as a member of Vistage was the MBA I didn't have. I remained in Vistage up until the pandemic. During my time there I literally dreamed up and learned how to sell my business, went through the process of buying multiple businesses and still have the friends I met up to this day. It was an immensely powerful time in my life when I was a member of the group. During those monthly meetings, I would expose myself and my business during the eight-hour meetings, and I was held accountable by my peers.

Once a year they would come through and interview all your leadership team without you in the room. They would ask them questions such as, what is going well with the company? What's the strategy moving forward? What areas are a weakness for the CEO?

After the interview, they would not tell me what happened, but instead would present it to the group during the next meeting as a case study. Their knowledge and expertise allowed them to give me tips such as moving employees around within the company where they could utilize their full potential. They also would advise me to be on the lookout when my plans were to double my business while one of my best employees, who was on the top of their game, was on the verge of succession.

The peers in that group continuously pushed me to become better. I believe my membership was the main reason I was able to hit so many of my goals. Vistage is still around and is a huge organization that is very impactful. They operate in 600 countries globally.

As outside business consultants they can provide perspective from an unbiased, unvested point of view. They have no emotional attachment to your business, do not know the owner's personal viewpoints or the conversations that go on within your company. This gives them the ability to point out blind spots that an entrepreneur would not be able to see because they are too focused on the day-to-day operations. This is different from consultants that you hire because they have a vested interest in your business.

After joining the larger business group, it helped me shift my goals from making my financial goals, to focusing on what my employees wanted and needed and making my team successful. During my one-on-ones with the advisors, I shifted my focus to what my employees reported to them and their needs. Nobody works for a company to make the owner successful; this is something I talk about all the time. Employees are not tethering themselves to your company for you to become wealthy. I did not do it when working for someone and I needed to realize that my employees wouldn't do it working for me.

One day (well before the pandemic where flexibility has become a paramount employee retention tool), an employee of mine informed me that they wanted to go down to a part-time role. I looked at him and was like, "umm no, you're a full-time creative." One of the Vistage coaches happened to walk into my business right after my meeting with the employee. When he asked me what was going on and I shared how the employee wanted to go to part-time and I told them no, he said, "Well I guess if you can decide that then they can leave the company too."

Perplexed, I looked at him and told him that I did not want the employee to leave the company, to which he replied, "If you don't figure out how to make it exciting for your employees and find a way to take all their obstacles and turn them into goals, then they will go somewhere else and work for someone who can." I like to stay on the offense and don't like playing defense, so this helped me change my perspective.

I believe most people have a tough time articulating what exactly it is that they want. As a leader, our job is to hear what is not being said and what your employees aren't articulating. Know that your employees often think that you can understand what they are going through even when you yourself may not have a clue. You as an owner could be thinking everything is going great, only to be met one day with a letter of resignation from an employee. The employee may think they had a prior conversation with you regarding what is going on in their lives and you remember the interaction as a brief exchange where you passed each other in the hallway.

Understand that not everyone is going to be direct with the owner about what they are seeking or dealing with. It takes a lot, but you must learn about your people and try to draw out from them what it is they need by asking questions. Keep that in mind when having daily interactions. Knowing that I did not want to lose that employee, made me come to a compromise that allowed him to get what he needed to achieve his personal goals.

I almost missed one of the most impactful experiences in my life and business all because I did not want to take the time out. I felt that I did not have the time to invest each month and underestimated how that one action could have tremendous results. Take notes from me, if you are an entrepreneur or business owner and are looking to grow, you must take time out and work on your business. Find ways to learn from others in your market, especially the large companies. Work and find out how to get a seat at the table.

If you don't have a mentor, coach, or peer group, I urge you to check into it. Mastermind groups are an excellent way to learn about your market. Continuing education is another opportunity where you can surround yourself with peers that are on the same journey that you're on. Find the secret sauce. The growth of your business depends on it. **Keep in mind that the bigger the mindset, the bigger the results**. Unless your business is about to close, do not let fear hold you back.

By constantly learning in the field of your craft, you obtain information that will continue to help you individually as well as professionally. If you don't take anything else away from this chapter, take away how important it is to always remain a student of the game. Lead with a servant mentality because if you help people with their goals, your goals always get taken care of.

As a student of the game, it allows me to share some information that can help you to work on your business as opposed to working in your business. I have compiled a list of common myths entrepreneurs often have, characteristics and qualities they possess and some common mistakes.

Myth #1: "Success is all about having a great idea."
Reality: While a great idea is valuable, **execution and implementation** are equally important. A brilliant concept alone does not guarantee success. It requires careful planning, effective execution, adaptability and a focus on addressing customer needs.

Myth #2: "Failure is a bad thing."
Reality: Failure is a natural part of the business journey and can provide valuable learning experiences. Many successful entrepreneurs and business leaders have faced failures along the way. It's crucial to embrace failures, learn from them and use the knowledge gained to iterate and improve your approach.

Myth #3: The customer is always right."
Reality: While customer satisfaction is important, it doesn't mean that customers are always right. Sometimes, customers have unrealistic expectations or make unreasonable demands. Businesses need to find a balance between accommodating customers' needs and making decisions that align with their overall vision and values.

Myth #4: "Entrepreneurs are born, not made."
Reality: Entrepreneurship is a combination of innate traits and learned skills. While some individuals may have certain predispositions that lead them to entrepreneurship, anyone can develop entrepreneurial skills through education, experience and personal growth. Entrepreneurship is a journey of continuous learning and improvement. AND BEING NIMBLE. Don't hide being the Big Company Mentality.

Myth #5: "Working longer hours equals higher productivity." Reality: The number of hours worked doesn't necessarily correlate with productivity. Working longer hours without proper breaks and rest can lead to burnout and decreased efficiency. It's more important to focus on working smarter, prioritizing tasks and maintaining a healthy work-life balance to maximize productivity and well-being.

Qualities and Characteristics that Entrepreneurs should follow include:

- **Goal Setting and Planning**: Successful individuals are known for setting clear, specific and measurable goals. They establish both short-term and long-term objectives and create actionable plans to achieve them. By setting goals and creating a roadmap, successful people maintain focus and direction, making steady progress towards their desired outcomes.
- **Continuous Learning and Personal Growth**: Successful people prioritize lifelong learning and personal development. They have a growth mindset and actively seek opportunities to expand their knowledge and skills. This can involve reading books, attending seminars, workshops, seeking mentorship or pursuing formal education. Continuous learning

enables them to adapt to new challenges, innovate and stay ahead of the curve.

- **Discipline and Productivity**: Successful individuals understand the importance of discipline and effective time management. They establish routines, prioritize tasks and eliminate distractions to maximize productivity. They set deadlines, delegate when necessary and maintain a strong work ethic. By being disciplined and organized, they can accomplish more in less time and achieve their goals efficiently.
- **Networking and Relationship Building:** Building a strong network and nurturing relationships is a habit of successful people. They understand the value of connecting with others, collaborating and seeking mutually beneficial partnerships. They actively engage in networking events, industry conferences and social platforms to expand their professional circle and create opportunities for growth and collaboration.

Top 5 Mistakes that All Entrepreneurs Make

- **Inadequate market research:** Failing to conduct thorough research before launching a business is a major mistake. Without understanding the target market, customer needs and the competitive landscape, entrepreneurs risk developing products or services that do not meet market demands.

- **Poor financial management:** Neglecting proper financial management is a significant pitfall. Entrepreneurs should establish sound financial systems, monitor cash flow, track expenses, revenues and have a clear understanding of their financial position. Ignoring these aspects can lead to financial instability and potential failure.
- **Lack of focus and trying to do everything:** Entrepreneurs often have numerous ideas and opportunities, which can lead to a lack of focus. Trying to pursue too many directions at once can dilute resources, stretch the team thin and hinder overall progress. It's crucial to prioritize and focus on the most promising opportunities.
- **Ignoring customer feedback:** Overlooking customer feedback is a common mistake that can have adverse effects. Entrepreneurs should actively seek and listen to customer input to understand their needs, preferences and pain points. Ignoring or undervaluing customer feedback results in missed opportunities and decreased customer satisfaction.
- **Not building a strong team:** Trying to do everything alone or failing to hire the right talent is a mistake many entrepreneurs make. Building a strong team with

complementary skills and expertise is essential for success. Neglecting team building and talent acquisition can limit growth potential and hinder business development.

Takeaways

To summarize this chapter, always continue expanding your knowledge to work for your business. Take time to remove yourself from the driver's seat and inspect how your business is moving. If you notice any systems or issues that need to be improved, take the necessary steps to work towards that.

Connect with the right people and network to expand your knowledge of the industry. Consider a mentor, coach, consulting group or mastermind. It is up to you and you alone to learn what is needed so that you can take your business to the next level. You might be met with opposition from men who don't like the idea of a woman trying to lead to which I say, tell them to move over.

Have you ever stepped outside your business to inspect its operations and issues that need to be resolved?

What are ways that you can continue to educate yourself to expand your business?

Chapter 3

Marketing Versus Listening and Networking

"Smart brands don't just ride trend shifts. They start them."

Ann Hardy, writer and digital marketer

Marketing and networking are two very distinct aspects in business. Marketing is a strategic approach taken to promote your products or services to a large audience. The goal of marketing is to create awareness of your company, generate leads and ultimately turn those leads into customers. Marketing is all about taking action. There are many ways that you can market your business including online and offline marketing, print ads, commercials and content marketing.

Networking, on the other hand, is the process of building connections and relationships within your industry. This could be with peers, potential business contacts or colleagues to exchange information and opportunities. You network by hitting the pavement and putting yourself out there. Meet and connect with others through one-on-one meetings, social gatherings and online platforms.

Back in the day, business owners saw marketing as something needed for those who couldn't sell. There was this belief many business owners had that marketers were losers and salesmen were the kings. During that time, I was running this company and served as the general manager. We had a top division that helped our company drive annual sales of $500MM. Five hundred million dollars in sales is huge and bear in mind we did not spend any money on marketing. No marketing team, no commercials, no big advertising. This was a very big accomplishment.

At that time, in the nineties, the internet was just becoming known, so we had no website, no cellphone, no brochure and basically, we were providing custom solutions to which we would go out and talk a lot and somehow land those million-dollar deals. It was the right place at the right time because no way on earth could you ever sell millions of dollars in deals in today's age without having appropriate marketing material. We did no trade shows and basically our business was word of mouth and yet under my leadership, we got our division to $500MM annually.

Part of the reason we did so well is because our company had a distinct niche, and I am great at connecting with people. We would call on our retailers, who were everywhere in over fifty locations and through our working relationships I saw that our suppliers were some talkers. They would talk and talk and tell you everything you needed to know regarding many things in the business, more importantly who my next target was. I was exceptionally good at supplier relationships, talked to all the suppliers we distributed to and if I wanted to find out what customers were doing, they all knew and would tell me.

Because I was so friendly with and talked so often to my suppliers, most of my lead generations came from the very gossipy suppliers, who in our industry, love to brag about what they were doing. You can also speed up the pipeline by asking questions to better solve customers' problems. After learning this, I would go to business meetings and always ask questions and would never speak about my business. I have been known to be a naturally curious person but doing this also allows them to lay out all their problems.

We are in business to solve problems and to go after them. During every interaction, my sole focus was asking questions to determine what solution I could offer. Using this strategy helped me to close many deals. I would call suppliers into my office, one after another, most of the representatives would have a quota of how many people they had to see each week. I am always thinking about what solutions I can offer and how to connect the dots.

I had a supplier that came to me gloating that they sold bags to Victoria's Secret, and he was just bragging and telling everyone about the deal. I just sat and listened as he continued to go on about how their company had a price increase and if Victoria's Secret did not take their inventory out by September, they would not have a fourth quarter.

Little did he know that Victoria's Secret was so unhappy with how they were getting their bags distributed that they had ordered extra quantities to have on hand. They were having problems maintaining an adequate supply of bags for their customers. After hearing the situation, I realized that they needed a fulfillment partner, then I got into gear to solve their problem.

Business in America is all about selling solutions. If you're selling one thing in a box, you will not last. Whether you provide custom solutions, write books, create avatars or sell a product, customers will tell you what's broken if you just listen enough. After I heard about the problem, I got on the phone and connected with the player (Andy Neri!) who handled the supplies, scheduled a meeting and looked like a hero. Not only could I get you the products his company needed, but I could also get them to you fast.

That is how I would turn that little idea into our next multimillion dollar account. I shortcut five steps in the process all because one guy was bragging about what he was doing and literally gave me the roadmap. Listening to this industry was just like attending an MBA program. Even though I did not realize it, I was marketing my business from networking with others. My networking abilities got me the deal.

The lesson from that story is that relationships are everything. I made sure to nurture all the business relationships I had because I knew how important they were. I would send them birthday, Christmas and Hanukkah cards, pizza, candy, cakes, whatever I could to show them I cared. Since our relationships became so strong, they would often come into my office, and they would feel like they were having a coaching session. They would download all their stuff to me, and I would allow them to talk their heads off so I could get more leads and land deal after deal.

The people in your industry have prospects on clients that you are trying to get. You just need to hit the pavement, talk and network with others who have a vested interest in the industry that you are in. You can find out what companies aren't doing well, and they could possibly be acquisition targets or those who are doing well, and they can become companies that you could study. Look at their strategies to determine if your company could implement any in some way.

Through the relationships I nurtured I became a trusted advisor for many of my suppliers. If they asked me for something I would try my hardest to make it happen because I really needed them to be by my side. I believe that is the basis of marketing. It is branding, positioning and establishing a belief about a company. One of our associates left our company and ended up becoming one of our biggest competitors. The situation could have been compared to one of the most familiar feuds in American history that started during the Civil War and spanned across decades, the "Hatfield's and McCoy's."

He was a very salesy guy and always appeared to be closing deals or at least gave the impression that he was always closing deals. He would approach his prospects with a sense of urgency such as, "you better sign this deal before it goes away." He would go to other suppliers and always trash talk our company, saying that we were full of ourselves. Every time he met with the supplier, he never asked questions because he was too busy talking trash. He could have taken advantage of the connection and actively listened, instead he chose to gossip and talk. Some people loved him because they liked the hoopla and drama, however others saw right through him. It ended up not working out for him because his business could not keep up and as a result, over time, our company ended up buying his company.

We must realize that everyone is in sales. The ones that make mistakes are those who try to pull or push customers instead of those who attract customers. You do not want to be a pusher out of the gate. When you cram things down people's throats, it doesn't last. Remember we are in this for multi-decade relationships. **Remember that lifetime value of a customer concept.**

Don't risk relationships just for a sale and a transaction. Earl Taylor is a prominent real estate broker, and he has a saying that goes, "Nobody likes to be sold to, but everybody likes to buy." This means that you must make sure that your customers and clients see the value in the product that you are offering or selling and that they are satisfied. You want to hit your goals; however, you never want to push someone to buy. If you're planting enough seeds, something will eventually come to harvest, whether it be today or in five years from now.

The art of being a great conversationalist helps with your networking. You can become better at marketing yourself and your business by remembering to always ask questions and limit how much you talk about yourself. You should follow the 80/20 rule that is also known as the "Pareto Principle". This concept, named after economist Vilfredo Pareto, states that 80% of consequences come from 20% of the causes, asserting an unequal relationship between inputs and outputs.

The Pareto Principle serves as an observation that some things in life will not always be distributed evenly. I use this principle when having conversations with others and let the client speak 80 percent of the time and only talk 20 percent of the time. Remember to ask the 3 "W'" questions that are, what, why and who. What issue can I help them with? Why do I want to help them? Who am I talking to?

I was out the other day with one of my salespeople and we had a meeting with a client. When the client arrived, she started sharing with us her excitement after coming back from Paris and just as she was starting her story, my associate interrupted her saying, "I am going to Paris too!" My salesperson completely took the air out of the client's sail and changed the focus from the customer to herself. I kept my cool, but gave her a look as if to say, "Are you kidding me?!"

Once we were alone, I told her the meeting went well but, even though I understood her excitement about Paris, she should never interrupt a client in the middle of a story again. We are there to pump up the customer and make them feel great and important. They need to feel like the most important person in the room and we need to always keep the spotlight on the customer. The customer was cut off and we did not get to hear what her favorite part of Paris was.

Considering I have lived in Paris many times in my life, I could have thought up over twenty questions to ask, asked to see pictures and could have connected with her over our love of Paris. Unfortunately, we did not get the opportunity to do that. It was a learning experience for my salesperson.

Gemini Molding was one of my key suppliers at the last company I started and was up for sale. Since I worked with them before I knew the business. I knew enough about it to be dangerous. I also knew that the market was shifting. Speed and lead-times were being compressed. I needed to be in control of production. Being in control of my production was vital because not just my customers, but all customers wanted products faster. “Amazon speed” was starting to be a thing. People were beginning to be accustomed to ordering products and receiving them fast such as the next day or even the same day of the purchase.

Customers would come to me with crazy request like, “I need a four-foot pink Christmas tree and I want it to be glittery because it’s going in my Victoria Secret stores. Oh, and can you show me a sample by tomorrow?” I would think, is this person real? What fantasy world are they in? A world where I can snap my fingers and a custom-colored tree with glitter would magically appear? They were out of touch with reality because America does not make custom pink Christmas trees. I would have to go to China to get something like that and shipping from China is going to take longer than one day.

Situations like this would happen day in a day out. That caused me to think about being a manufacturer supplier. The magic would be if I had control over production. I knew that if I had the ability to talk to my customers, determine what it is they want and be able to come back the next day with a sample would change the game for me. The only way that I would be able to do this is if I held all the cards and was able to walk out of my shop and tell my guys what it is I need, show them a prototype and have them make a sample for the customer.

The purchase of Gemini Builds It! happened super-fast. I went to the owner of the business, made an offer and purchased it. I did not exactly follow the chain of acquisitions in that deal, but sometimes you have to jump on an opportunity when you see it. I made a deal that wedged the seller in a corner. The seller was an older man, around the age of eighty and he was nervous about the entire process. He probably thought, if he did not take this deal, it was going to expire, and I was basically saying that indeed it would expire. A clause was placed in the contract that stated in ninety days I would buy his company and if I didn't the seller would have to pay a breakup fee. Never in the history of acquisitions has this happened.

This is something that I have never heard of, and he ended up signing the contract. He was too cheap to pay the $50,000 breakup fee so I knew that he would end up going through with the sale. They were a smaller company, not very sophisticated, when I received their financials, they looked bad.

Some concern started to grow that I may have paid too much for that company. Even with my initial concern, I saw the potential to use this business as my platform company. It was a huge building with a broad set of talent and a lot of bandwidth. They also were underutilized, and employees were only working like half of one shift when the business could have employees work various shifts and keep the building open 24 hours.

I shared my plans for the company, how I planned to grow it to six times the production and wanted to create various value streams. I expressed concern about the purchase price and wondered if I spent too much money. They all told me that sometimes you have to make an expensive buy to get you where you're going. Thinking back on the purchase, now I know that I paid a fair price. I believe networking helped provide me with the knowledge needed for me to make a sound purchase of Gemini Molding. The business soon changed to Gemini Builds It, and we branded Showcase Acrylics. Our company is **Gemini Builds It!** and **Showcase Acrylics**.

We are a top producer in the art world for artists and produce bases and pedestals for museums and institutions that display items, along with a lot of other products. Acrylics are the top half of all our museum displays. The bottom is a wood pedestal, and the top is an acrylic vitrine. Our company today is combined of all the manufacturing you would need to create custom décor and environments for businesses.

Takeaways

The main takeaway is to make sure when you talk to people in your industry that you do more listening than talking. Remember the Pereto Principle. By listening, you have an opportunity to find some of your best deals and information.

If you just listen to others, especially those who can't shut their mouths, it can decrease the work you have to do in the sales process. You can skip the discovery process by vetting the client. Networking benefits you in many ways. Keep this in mind when networking for your business. Actively listen and remember the importance of nurturing your professional relationships.

- In what ways can you actively listen and network in your industry to expand your business?
- How are your conversation skills?
- Do you listen to reply or listen to understand?
- How are you currently marketing your business?

Chapter 4

Age is Bullshit

"Women grow radical with age. One day an army of gray-haired women may quietly take over the Earth."

Gloria Steinem, American Journalist

Ageism, or age discrimination is something that occurs quite often in modern business. With baby boomers leaving the workforce and more companies being led by younger individuals, a youth-centric culture has been created. Some employers hold biases or stereotypes about older workers and believe that they are less adaptable, less energetic, or less productive. There are some employees who even feel this way about their older coworkers. We don't consider the possibility that older employees could be knowledgeable, dedicated, focused and driven.

This is crazy to me because in our society we have created a glass ceiling that tries to stop people from working as they get older. What is even crazier is that older individuals have started to believe that themselves. Some believe that they age out of certain jobs or that they are not as productive as they get older. I think people age out because they are not doing what they love to do and are not pursuing their passion. They don't like the career they are in and may have never liked the career. The lack of fulfillment makes them want to stop working.

Age is such a BS thing. As an entrepreneur there is no shelf life, and you only get better with time. Sometimes, coworkers and family will come to me to tell me how I am almost 60 years old, how good I am doing, and ask if I am ready to retire. I usually look at them like they are crazy and reply, "Why? I feel like a kindergartener!" I feel like I am at the starting blocks of my greatness and personally think in the next ten years that I will hit four times the numbers that I have done in the last decade.

It's only up from here and there is nothing that can stop me. I've gone through my journey. There are so many more things I want to accomplish, and it's crazy for me to think about retiring because I take care of myself to beat my age and have a lot of life and learning left. The thing is, I love what

I do. I love solving problems and building businesses, and the difference now is that I have the wisdom to know how to do it better and faster. I also have the money to invest in more ventures than when I was younger and now if I make a mistake, who cares?

There is no fear of failure to stop me from trying new things and ideas. Although I do what I love, there are aspects of the job that I do not like to do. At my age I have earned the right to not have to do what I don't want to do. The duties that I don't want to do actively get taken off my plate. If I don't love a part of my job, I will hire a replacement to do it. I remain focused on executing my genius and my true gifts. The things that can be delegated, I hand off to others on my team. Then there are certain things that cannot be delegated and that is what I refer to as my genius. Those are the things that I enjoy, am good at and produce a lot of value for the companies we serve.

Right now, at fifty-seven years old, I feel better than I did at thirty years old by a long shot. I am making sure to take care of my machine and I stay ready for a race all the time. There are many reasons for that, but mostly because at thirty years old I didn't have the confidence that I have now. Many may wonder what confidence has to do with feeling good. Confidence has everything to do with feeling good! In my thirties, I remember that I was so stressed out. I was stressed out because I was clear about my vision for my future and very clear about the way I wanted it to look.

I created the vision for my life and yet I was trapped in a company where I was building freedom for someone else. That was my fault. I didn't have the confidence to make the move that I knew I so desperately wanted. I did not have the confidence to make a change, put my freedom, family and finances at risk and pull the trigger to tell my boss, "I quit."

Now, even though I still have some stress in my life, in no way is it like when I was in my thirties, because now, I work for my own freedom. I take care of myself better now as well. I value my health and my sleep. Making sure to eat well and to practice mindfulness are also important in caring for yourself. Like a vintage car that has been restored and runs better after all the work was put in, I feel better now than when I was built. Self-care is necessary if you are working on maintaining youth and energy.

The one percent rule is something I follow in relation to improving myself. This principle encourages you to work on your goals, plans and self-improvement one percent at a time instead of setting monumental goals and plans that can overwhelm you. Following the one percent rule, I monitor and measure everything in my life, from my diet, to exercise, sleep, work, family, etc. The one percent compounds over the years, I get even better and who knows, I may run a triathlon. Who knows what I can do!

Back when I was in my older thirties, I knew I wanted to work for myself and that I desired my freedom, but for some reason I just could not take the first step. At that time, I was working for an employer who one could call a “bed check” employer, meaning that if he could not see you, he did not trust you. He wanted to know what I was doing at all times. If I wasn’t on a plane or in the office, in his mind I was not be working. My days were long, I would work twelve hours a day, from seven in the morning to seven in the evening, and I absolutely pulled my weight.

One day, one of my sons, Briggs, was sick and needed to go to the doctor. This was before COVID 19 and before remote working became a thing. That morning I went to my boss, told him that my son needed to go to the doctor, and I was going to take him the next day. I told him that I would come in after taking my son and should arrive at work around nine in the morning. His reply to me was, “Can’t you have that lady do that?” That lady he was referring to was my nanny and no, she could not do that. I had my children so that I would be at every doctor’s appointment, every single activity, every single game. I realized that his response was not going to get any better as my children grew older and their lives became busier. That’s I realized that I could not work for him and live the life that I wanted.

That night, I was having a conversation with my husband, who had just completed his MBA and was working in the automotive industry. He was telling me that he wasn't really into his boss and before he finished the sentence, I cut him off and said, "That's it, I'm going to do it, I'm going to give my notice and quit my job." He asked me why, and that's when it all came out. I told him I just couldn't do it anymore and it was not going to work with me having to raise our children. My husband looked at me, gave me a kiss on the forehead, told me to do it and that I had his full support.

Larry had to have been a little concerned about my decision. If your wife is making that kind of money and you're a financial guy, you're going to be focused on the numbers. He asked me what my business plan was to which I replied, "Don't worry, I'm going to make one up." I will never forget the puzzled expression on his face as I told him not to worry. He literally just completed his master's program in Business Administration and here I was telling him I was going to quit my job to start a business without a plan. He told me, "Worrying is what I do."

Even though I understood where he was coming from, I was going to bet on myself and make sure that my plan worked. That was the beginning of the end of my time at that company. From the moment I had the conversation with my husband, I started making plans to leave. My mind was made up. The next morning before getting on a business call, I tore a piece of paper out of a notebook and wrote down my one-page business plan. I told my husband that I was going to sell $10MM in the first year.

My husband, being the smart man that he is, created a more realistic goal for me and crossed out the ten million dollars and wrote down that I would sell one million dollars. I asked if he changed the amount because of his lack of confidence in me and he replied, “Who the heck can produce $10MM in sales in year one?” I wanted to answer him and say, “I can” however, I just decided to take his advice about hitting a realistic goal and the rest is history. Since then, my husband has been a great supporter, my business partner, and has stood behind me, backing me all the way.

I had it all mapped out when I was going to give my notice and receive my final commissions with the plan of investing the money. I was afraid of having regrets and feeling like a failure by leaving my seven-figure job where I had momentum and had people to carry my bags! In essence, I had tenure and worked there 17 years to build it. It wouldn’t have been an easy situation either way when I left.

Going forward without an income was precarious. I was not scared of losing that, but scared of failure and having regrets that I hadn’t filled my potential. I might have regretted that I didn’t do a bigger thing in my life. A regret that I didn’t listen to the inner entrepreneurial voice.

The day I left my job was the scariest experience, even though I had my exit strategy clearly mapped out. I walked into Andy McKenna's office, my boss and I told him that I was going to leave the company. Do you want to know what his answer to me was? He replied, "No, you're not." That is what his answer was. He really did not take me seriously. We went back and forth for a short time, with me telling him I was leaving and him telling me I wasn't. Eventually, I told him that I had to leave and was still going to be friends with him. I explained to him that I had a vision of what I wanted to do, and I had to do it for myself. I wanted to be a business owner and there was no way that could happen with me working for them. The company was family owned, which I could respect, but there was no way that I could buy in to become part owner, so I was going to create my own business that I could own and operate.

Our conversation took place on June 1, 2005, and three weeks had gone by since informing him of my plans to resign. In that three-week time frame, he hadn't spoken to me once. He just iced me and would avoid me in passing. The situation was a little awkward to say the least. I could not understand that because I had been an exceptional employee during my time there and had enough consideration for him to give him a heads up. My last day at the company was set for July 5th. Eventually, he came to me and asked if I could stay until the end of the fiscal year, which was at the end of September, he would give me an incentive. I agreed to stay but asked him who was taking my place; he did not have an answer.

The end of September started to roll around and again I asked him if he was going to announce to everyone that I was leaving. He said "no." He had no intentions of informing anyone. I wanted to reach out to our suppliers and inform them that I was resigning but did not because, after all, it was not my company.

Once our suppliers found out, most of them were ticked and rightfully so. They thought that I was leaving them right at the peak of the busy Christmas season, high and dry with no replacement. Many were furious and could not deal with the change without a succession plan. I could understand how they felt because I had worked with some of those suppliers for over a decade. We had built strong, lasting relationships, but at the end of the day, I did not own the company and that was not my responsibility, it was that of the company owner.

It is the employer's responsibility to inform customers when key employees are leaving the company and not the employee. That falls on the company and their public relations. I just wish that he would have handled that situation in a better way and considered the suppliers. Relationships matter and are crucial to your success. Try not to burn bridges, because you never know when you might need someone again in the future. If you leave a company, make sure you do it with grace, because it always comes back to you. I tried to stay as long as I could and worked my tail off until my last day there. The incentive that my boss paid me for staying is what I used to fund my company, even though I did not agree with how my boss handled my resignation, I was grateful for the excellent compensation.

My coworkers and others were excited for me, but excited in an odd way. They would look at me as if they wanted to ask why me why I would leave a job where I was vice president and general manager of a large company. Why, with two small kids, would I risk it all? I am not exactly sure myself, but my decision to take a chance turned out to be a big, interesting success.

CDW Merchants is the company that I started after writing it down on that paper for Larry. My goal was to start, build and sell a business within ten years. Writing it down made it real. Again, I am not sure where I got the idea, but that was my desire.

When I made the decision to leave Schwarz, my age was the furthest thing from my mind. Since then, I have expanded my friends to include more young people because they give me clarity. People who believe their age stops them from doing things they like are people that I do not want to surround myself with. So, my older friends are the ones who embrace that mindset. When I started networking and working with people who are younger than me, I shared my perspective on life having gone through the journey. I like engaging with them, I feel like they listen to me, and I have all this wisdom to share.

When I was their age, everything in my life seemed like a life-or-death situation. I felt like I was protecting little birds and things felt monumental. In hindsight, I realized that everything was going to be all right. I see people my age that talk about retirement and, I think, not me! I would still like to be around for a long time and have so many things that I want to do. It seems like you blink twice, and the kids are grown and out of the house.

While raising a family, it doesn't always feel that way, because every day can feel like a marathon, you run around all day, sleep at night, then wake up to do the same thing all over again. Often, I come across professionals in their mid-thirties who are making major moves. They are building empires and I often mentor them. I try to show them that everything is going to be okay and give them pats on the back when needed and strive to get them to just enjoy the ride. When I was their age, I would have loved to have someone mentor me. Proximity is power. You can become a powerful person when you spend time with powerful people. The same thing applies if you are trying to lose weight or stop smoking. You don't want to continue to be around those who frequent all you can eat buffets or hang out in bars with those who smoke. **You are the average of everyone you hang around with and spend your time with. Choose wisely!**

If I were constantly around people who felt old and had dead dreams, then eventually the energy would transfer, and I would start to feel old, and my dreams would die. Knowing this, be very aware of the energy that you are around. Guard your energy with your life, because if you surround yourself with people who don't constantly move the needle one percent forward in whatever way you're working on, you're going backwards.

Takeaways

Let's end on this note, your age should not deter you from pursuing your dreams. Age is an asset, it establishes relationships because the longer you know a person, the more you know about them and strengthens your relationship.

With age comes wisdom. People's concept of "too late" is often subjective. When it comes to personal fulfillment, it is never too late if you still have the right state of mind and can do the job. Nurture your relationships and don't burn bridges.

Take care of your body and your body will take care of you. Guard your energy and surround yourself with those who are improving themselves.

Regardless of how old or young you are, keep pursuing your dream!

- How do you feel at the current age that you are right now in your life?
- Do you feel like a well-oiled machine or a weakened vessel?
- Have there been any self-limiting beliefs that you have held because of your age?

Chapter 5

Be a YES Company

"We are not interested in the possibilities of defeat; they do not exist."

Queen Victoria

As a business owner, it's important to set yourself apart from others. To do this, it is important for you to understand your target audience, their needs and preferences. Once you determine that, you can tailor your strategies and offers accordingly. This is valuable because once you set your business apart from the crowd, it will benefit you. Your company will have a competitive advantage by establishing loyal customers, which leads to long-term success. Setting yourself apart may involve differentiating your products and services from all others, providing exceptional customer service, offering customizable solutions, specializing in a specific niche or incorporating innovative technology.

From the moment I started my business, I knew that I had to set my company apart from the rest. Customizing is what I do, and I have tried to never shy away from a challenging client request. I want my clients to not just be satisfied, but to love the products we provide. By catering to the customer's needs, it has helped my business remain successful.

One of the big clients is a global marketing wizard and world class photographer. He was a former investment manager turned creative and when you talk about someone being free from money, he is the person you are referring to. The starving artist lifestyle was not a concept in his brain. His niche was taking breathtaking pictures of everything from wildlife, indigenous communities, nature and more. My company was able to contract with him because someone else messed up. One day, I received a call from my client, Arica (Hilton Contemporary), asking if we could take on his job that the other company messed up which needed to be completed in 24 hours. They explained that the client was in a time crunch and asked if I could stop by to meet him.

At the meeting, I was introduced to a charming Scottish man, whose pictures are exquisite and awe-inspiring to say the least. The pictures start at thirty thousand dollars apiece and I thought to myself, this is my type of guy. After speaking with him, I learned he grew globally very quickly and through social media and a mega gallery distribution channel. Due to his growth and the global distribution of these pictures, he needed a company that could keep up with his demands.

When your company is growing, make sure that your supplier is growing as fast, if not greater than you are. If not, you're going to have problems. The company that he was using was slow and clunky and he was ready for a change. My company was able to provide a solution to his problem and he was quite satisfied.

That next day, when meeting him to provide his framed work, I invited him to come view our plant. He looked at me as if he wanted to say, "Who are you again? You did one thing for me, and you think I want to see your plant?" Well at least that's how it felt. He respectfully declined due to work demands and I did not push the issue at that moment.

I continued to stay connected with him and started doing a few things for him. Whatever I needed to do to nurture that relationship, I did. Every time we spoke, I invited him to view our plant. I knew that I would eventually wear him down. The next time that he came to town, I told him that I valued his time and to make it more convenient, arranged to have a helicopter fly us from Chicago to my plant. We could get there in around thirty minutes and he would still have time to go about his day.

The look of total fear washed across his face as he told me that he does not ride in helicopters. Here is this tall guy who literally walks around lions and puts his face in tiger's mouths all the time to take breathtaking pictures and he is scared to get in a helicopter? After going back and forth for a minute, he eventually agrees to come view the plant but passes on the helicopter and opts to have his chauffeur drive him instead. That was perfectly fine with me, I understand some people just don't do heights in a small aircraft and, at the end of the day, how he got there didn't matter. What mattered was just getting him there.

When David arrived at our company, we had everything set out for him. I had all my employees dressed in a T shirt that we custom-made that said Yarrow, which was is his name with a lion on the back with the words "Ready to Roar."

He was genuinely impressed and after looking around our plant told me how he underestimated me and thought my company was very small. He was not expecting me to open the door to a fifty thousand square foot, twenty-four-foot-high building. The machines were moving, people were working, and he looked at me and said, "Holy shit, well done." This is why I always stress the importance of face-to-face meetings. All the marketing in the world cannot replace in-person interactions and visuals.

After touring our facility, he walked to the front with me and said he wanted to ask me a question. Eager to gain him as a regular client, I told him, "Whatever it is, we can get the job done." He asked how long it would take my company to get him a quote for freight. I told him we could get it done in ten minutes and he was amazed. The company that he was currently doing business with was taking three days. He told me that he wanted us to perform some of his logistics.

Taking beautiful pictures is one thing, but how we get them to the high-net-worth customers and onto their walls is a whole separate arrangement. The whole experience is created once the artwork is unveiled and lifted onto the wall and looks perfect in the living room.

That part of his business, he explained, needed help. I knew, for a fact, that his custom framing needed more support because of his huge growth. We discussed our logistics and got his order done. Of course, when I first agreed to do the job, in my head I thought, "oh shit," but he would have never known that. We got the job done!

Later down the line, Arica and David hosted a charity event which we attended. By the end of the event, he raised a ton of money for charity. When he got up to say his thank you speech, he included our team. After thanking his family and colleagues, he says, "I want to thank Courtney and her team because they are the biggest 'yes' people I know." That has to be one of the highest compliments we have received in our company.

David explained that he is from Scotland and in Scotland it's a whole bunch of what you can't do. He went on to express how he is currently in America and America is supposed to be the land of endless opportunity and yet there weren't a lot of companies that say yes to everything. There were times that he came to me with difficult requests, such as needing thirteen pieces completed in one evening and delivered to Miami by noon the next day.

David said that the highest compliment he could give about my company was that every challenge that was thrown at us, we knocked it out of the park. That was a proud moment not just for me, but for my entire team. Our teamwork, dedication and hard work made the client extremely happy.

We ended up becoming a key supplier. This opportunity was given to us all because we said yes, every single time they had a request, while others were saying no. That client trusted me and my company, we became a go-to, an extension of his business and not just a supplier. This monumental business relationship started all because I was able to say yes.

Life gets so much better and gives you a lot more opportunities when you surround yourself with yes people. The type of people who believe in getting the job done. Many people struggle with this because of the fear of not being able to produce. "Atychiphobia" is defined as a fear of failure. Many people who have atychiphobia have an ingrained belief that they are not or will not be good enough. The term sounds confusing, however there are many people who experience extreme fear of failure, worry and negative thoughts when faced with achieving a goal.

When hiring employees, you hire for attitude and train for skill. Make sure you hire "yes" people. No one wants to be around naysayers and negative people all day. People want to be around someone who can take advantage of opportunities. When clients are overwhelmed, make them happy. When you work with nothing but yes people and they are faced with a challenge, they have the attitude of let's figure it out.

If your team has a yes culture, giving them a complex task to accomplish is like being the igniter to gas their fire. When working with David, he would come to us with what could be considered minor problems, that weren't exactly in the field of what we did at our company, I would handle the issue for him to allow him to focus on his genius. I would tell him, "You don't need to focus on this petty stuff, you go out there and take more pictures so I can do more framing."

Once you develop that trust with your client, you guard it with your life. My attitude of striving to make my clients happy, my willingness to take on a challenge and my commitment to quality work are what attract new, high-quality clients. My ability to be a "yes" company is what keeps the client.

"Your attitude, not your aptitude, will determine your altitude."

Zig Ziglar

Understand that, despite wanting to be a "yes" company, you will get hit with many "nos" along the way. You don't want to take no for an answer, but still understand that sometimes opportunities take time to mature. Trust me, I have heard many "nos" in my career. Remember how originally, I got a helicopter for David to visit my site?

Before I got the helicopter, I discussed the idea with my husband and remember him asking me, "How much is that going to cost just for him to get a ride to the plant?" True, I took a chance, but with big risks comes big rewards. Here was a man, who had turned me down repeatedly, however, I did not let that stop me.

After the helicopter invitation, David told me that I was the best business of all his service providers. He could tell by my approach that we were not just some mom-and-pop shop but the pick of the litter. He was impressed, and if I do say so myself, I would have been too. The whole situation was bad ass.

Let this be your inspiration to be creative. If you ask for a meeting and someone says no, realize there are a million different ways to get things done. There is a saying in the south, that there is more than one way to skin a cat. If one way does not work, then think of another.

Takeaways

- Be consistent and more creative than your competitors.
- The make-or-break is all about creativity and speed.
- You must be more creative, work faster than the rest and be a "yes" company!
- How can you make your business stand out from the rest?
- What are ways that you can before more creative to gain business?

Chapter 6

Pandemic Acrylic

"We learn the way, on the way."

Shannon Kaiser

The onset of COVID 19 struck the world by storm in late 2019. The virus spread globally and had a major effect on everyone. We all had to learn how to adapt to a new normal with school, work and everyday interactions. Businesses were impacted by shutdowns, leaving many owners scrambling to pivot their operations to meet changing demands. Thousands of businesses ended up having to close their doors due to the lack of business. Those that did make it through were the ones who learned how to be innovative and flexible. It was the survival of the fittest and you had to be strong to survive.

Prior to the full COVID 19 pandemic that struck the nation, I recall a conversation I was having with Gene Faut, one of my past Vistage peers. He was telling me how a large amount of people were getting sick from a virus and it was causing many events to get canceled. He personally had already lost seven million dollars in revenue from a trade show he was hosting that got canceled.

This was early 2020 and COVID 19 had not been made a public emergency at that time. People were starting to hear about a virus that many were contracting. It had not reached America in full force yet and most people were still going about business as usual. Despite the lack of immediate concern in America, I did not take it lightly. When people who are smarter and more successful than me say something, I take heed.

After our conversation, I went back to my office and went online to look up what was going on globally. At that time, I saw that the virus was hitting Italy hard, and I noticed online that many of the pictures showed customers who had begun eating behind curved pieces of acrylic that separated them from other patrons. Out of all the pictures I looked at, showing people with masks and gloves on in grocery stores, the main thing that stood out to me was the acrylic.

Since we manufacture acrylics, the wheels started spinning in my head and immediately, I got on the phone and called a meeting. During the emergency meeting I held, I told my team that we were about to be in for a heck of a ride and to buckle up. I saw the potential to excel, and nothing was going to stop us.

February 1, 2020, I started calling around and asking about the pandemic and everyone I spoke to was saying that they would just wait and see how things played out. Personally, I have never been the wait and see type of person, so I kept doing my research online. While scrolling I was noticing that acrylic was being used in the grocery stores in Italy to separate the patrons. First it was restaurants and now it's grocery stores. That was another sign.

I reached out to my marketing department and got on the phone with the distributor for Whole Foods. After securing a meeting, I met with Whole Foods and informed them that the pandemic was here and asked how they planned to protect their customers. At that time, I was told that Whole Foods did not need any acrylic safety equipment, okay no big deal. Since I don't burn bridges, I thank them for their time. Two days later, on a Saturday morning at 6:30 a.m. I received a phone call from the representative that handles Costco stores located about an hour north of me.

He asked me if I had acrylic and I answered with a yes. He told me that he needs sneeze guards and would need them to be delivered to his stores on Monday. The call took place on Saturday, and he needed thousands of acrylic sneeze guards produced in under two days. Up until this point, I had never heard of sneeze guards before in my life, just like the average person, because they weren't a popular item. I did not let the representative know that. Because I was a "yes" company, I told him that we made them. He explained how they would need to be custom cut along with all the other specifications he needed.

Monday morning, when I arrived at my business, I let all my employees know that we would be producing sneeze guards and the order needed to be completed and delivered that same day. The look on my employees' faces was priceless. Some looked scared, some bewildered and others shocked. I know it was a challenge for them, but because my team is a yes team, they got it done.

The next day Costco told Whole Foods and Whole Foods called and offered me the entire Midwest Territory, but the caveat was that I needed to have all the panels done by Thursday, which was a two day turn around. I told him, no problem. I knew information would eventually break, that something big was happening and my company was in better shape because I was prepared. I remember the Whole Foods representative asking me how on Earth was I going to get the order fulfilled in two days. I told him, "Even if my team and I had to stay up all night, we would get the order completed." Over the next two years I received many referrals from Whole Foods and Costco.

Every Costco had different managers and did not have margin sensitive orders. This meant that we were not making price sensitive products, they just needed orders fast. All the prepaid orders were custom-made and completed at the speed of sound. We ended up securing over one million dollars in orders within a 6-week period. I added in a lot of lead generations into the third week, calling all kinds of institutions, including colleges, chain stores, whoever I could think of who would need acrylic.

If I could do it again, it would be twice as big. Sometimes, you're good and sometimes, you're lucky and during the pandemic, I was **good and lucky**. I am good at listening to what is really being said. When someone is telling me a story, I know that there are many interconnected parts and must actively listen. When my friend first told me about what was happening, I took that information and ran with it. Our company probably was not the first to do this, however we did it slightly better than the rest. We were making custom solutions and not only that, but they also looked good. Our acrylic pieces were manufactured for the exact size and space needed. We looked for ways to lower our client's anxiety and that is exactly what we accomplished.

Despite the financial gains that the pandemic brought my company, there were some drawbacks as well. We had to downsize our staff to around thirty employees and that process involved us sitting down and going through our list of employees. Anyone who was negative and had a bad attitude had to go! Being a "yes" company requires you have "yes" employees. We were deemed essential workers by the government because we were producing acrylic and glass protection guards for companies.

At that time, there was an employee who worked for the company who had always had a bad attitude. He kept going around talking to other employees saying that the pandemic was fake, and we were not essential. Overall, just bringing down the morale of all the other employees. Another employee, who did not want to come to work unless she was in a "covered, germ resistant car." Both of those employees had to go. It was game time, and we were "balls to the wall" with acrylic orders. You are only as strong as your weakest link, and I could not afford to be weak.

We needed raw materials to handle business and that was a challenge at times. Our staff started working hybrid shifts and it felt like we were in the trenches. It became clear that **sometimes, where there is chaos, there is opportunity**. The pandemic provided so many opportunities for us to bond as a team. It really was a defining moment of what we were capable of. Looking back at our numbers and seeing how everyone was accountable for themselves makes me proud.

Good people figure shit out. A person's attitude could be considered the north star for who you chose to hire. Their attitude is everything. I want employees who are positive, energetic, forward-thinking and driven. Those types of employees are vital when you are betting on yourself. When I first got the idea to produce acrylic during the pandemic, I purchased a ton of the material.

My thought process was "What's the worst that could happen?" If it ended up not working out, I could always live in an acrylic house and I meant that. If I hadn't reacted when I did, we wouldn't have any business and may have had to shut down. I am a "no" failure type of person and what another person would consider as a failure, I see as an opportunity to reframe myself. I learned that I had to trust myself, took a bet and it paid off.

As women, we are equipped with our intuition which can be an advantage in our business and in life. According to Forbes, intuition in psychology is "nonconscious emotional information" that our bodies give us. It could also be thought of as a "gut feeling".

Psychology Today, published an article titled, *"What's Behind Women's Intuition,"* and in the article it describes how women have historically been the subordinate group in society. Due to being in this position, it has forced them to develop nonverbal and verbal skills. This ability is essential for effective communication. This gives us a competitive advantage with the ability to read people's emotions and use that to make informed decisions.

No doubt, the pandemic had a massive impact on my business, not just my personal life. I learned so many things, with the most important to be adaptable and ready to pivot at a moment's notice. To be responsible for helping so many businesses maintain social distancing and keeping their doors open, makes me proud.

I fully embraced change and uncertainty. I also know that I need to be constantly evaluating the market. There is no guarantee that another global pandemic won't occur. Stay ready so you don't have to get ready regarding your business. Embrace change when it occurs and ready to change directions if needed.

Takeaways

- How did the Pandemic affect your life and business?
- Have you ever been in a situation where you had to bet on yourself?
- If not, how can you currently bet on yourself as an entrepreneur and as a boss?

Chapter 7

Sale of My Company

"The rate of change has to be faster in your business than the outside world, or the end is near."

Courtney Wright

.

I started my first company, CDW Merchants, in 2006 and had it written on paper that I would start, build and sell a company in ten years. Five years into my business, I got a call from Mikel Eisenberg, who was my top competitor in my first sales job. He was a salesy type of guy, and we would always see each other in passing. He was the best of the best and I was the best of the best. I would make face-to-face sales calls and then would be on a plane going across the country and would see Mikel. We always had a competitive relationship with each other. He called to tell me that he was selling his company and thought that I should come and check it out. The year was 2011 when I went to a dinner and met with him as well as other businesspeople who were building a massive public holding company.

After that meeting, I was left with a decision to make. Because of my membership in Vistage, I knew enough about business to be dangerous. One of the chairmen at Vistage accompanied me and assisted us with the sale. He helped me with my letter of intent which was written in December 2011. Soon after that, I started having a gut feeling telling me to think longer about the decision. Not sure if that was out of fear or protection, but I listened and waited a little bit.

While still contemplating whether or not to sell my business I went to see one of our top customers to thank them for their business that year. She was a sweet representative, and I always enjoyed our conversations during business transactions. Our contact person informed me that she was diagnosed with a brain tumor. Hearing the news was shocking because this lady was very young, in her mid-thirties with so much more life to live.

She passed away shortly after I heard about her diagnosis. After hearing this tragic news, I was convinced that I should sign the LOI and sell our company. Her passing away was a game changer in my life. I realized that I had to sell, and time waits for no one. A bird in the hand is worth two in the bush as the old saying goes.

Despite my complex decision-making process, I came to the realization that everything in my life, aside from my husband Larry and our two children Briggs and Robert, is for sale. I don't give two shits about any of this materialistic stuff. If you have a perceived value on things, you must understand that others might not see it as you do. I do not believe in emotional attachments in business. Entrepreneurs should not get too emotional in business.

The rate of change has to be faster in your business than in the outside world and if not, the end is clear. Everything has a life cycle, and this includes energy, relationships, businesses and real estate. We must learn when to get in and know when to get out. Entrepreneurs must be innovative and have speed within their business.

Wealthy people plan how to make money in the future and not just right now. My way of thinking is similar, once I attained wealth, my focus became generational wealth. I am working on a fifty-year life plan. I do not ride the scarcity plane, it's abundance all day. A CEOs job is to look down at the train tracks to see what is coming. Do you need to increase your speed or slow down?

There is a process I have with my company where at the month's end, every manager compiles reports that we analyze. The reports allow us to see what went well, strengths, weaknesses and any opposing threats to the company. We discuss topics such as, “What we are doing with AI?” I ask the “what if” questions, such as, “What if there is an accident?” “What if one of our trucks need maintenance?” I pick the scab a little bit by asking questions, including the 3 “W’s”, to help my team think critically. I float ideas around to executives to prompt them into thinking in advance and becoming proactive. That allows us to formulate a plan for how to operate with any changes that need to be made. This is a process that we conduct every month.

Selling my business was the start of many profound changes in my career. I knew when the expiration date came up and because I was not emotionally attached, I could let it go. Consider this when making business deals. Never forget to ask the right questions. Don’t be afraid to make business moves, that move may be the one that changes your life.

Takeaways

- Are there any moves you have considered making but stopped?
- What stopped you?
- What is currently stopping you from making moves that you feel could change your life?

Chapter 8

Sometimes the Best Deals Are the Ones You Don't Do

"In business as in life, you don't get what you deserve, you get what you negotiate."

Dr. Chester Karrass

I started CDW merchants in 2006 and sold the business in 2012. I worked my last day at the public company in 2016. Towards the end of my time there, I had all my ducks in a row and the ending blocks were in place. I spent the last ten years saving and building my foundation and thought, "Oh shit, what am I going to do with myself?" That was a big question I had to ask myself, because even though I technically could have retired, it was not something I wished to do. After making the decision not to retire, I decided it would be a great idea to start a holding company.

This type of company is something that I have heard of and thought sounded sexy, I wasn't exactly sure what it was but thought, "Hey I could do that." A holding company is a company that buys businesses and holds them over the long term versus planning to run and sell them. A funny thing about me, I tend to start crazy stuff on a whim despite not knowing a lot about it. Even though I had little knowledge about holding companies, I decided that is what I would pursue next.

Going out and talking to owners about selling their company, having sold one myself versus buying one was a completely different process. I had previously been part of deal structures but was very light in due diligence although I knew enough to be dangerous. The company I purchased was familiar to me because I was one of their customers at CDW Merchants. They were a vendor of mine and I "thought" I knew what they did in their operations.

As a new owner, it seemed like I had fifty people working against me. The work culture was atrocious, and they did not know me, and their previous boss was no longer the owner. My husband would also come around and ask me questions, I'm sure it was probably a scary time for him. All I could tell him was, I just really wanted to do that deal. So, there I was, after just investing a butt load of money and now the company was bleeding money, even though over all it looked good on paper, the entire situation was a mess.

Around eighteen months later, I started to gain my footing and things started to smooth out, and there was a path lined out for me at the company, I tried to buy one of our competitors. It appeared to be a good deal, the client covered a region that our company could just take in and assimilate. It seemed like it would be a good synergistic move.

The company did the same thing we did and all I would have to do was strip the cost down. The owner of the company was a private equity guy, and he thought that his business was very valuable. The company was a smaller one and was not even making that much money. The owner kept forcing the sale and did not want me to focus on how much money the company had been making, he wanted me to focus on (and pay for the upside) potential. We ended up going back and forth for quite some time and could never agree on a purchase price.

The deal ended up fizzling out and I was a little bummed but kept pushing on. Shortly after, another customer approached me, he was a gentleman who owned an online business and was the type of person who hated dealing with customers and was overall NOT a people person. He had a framing business that he started online. I thought it was pretty genius that he recognized his skill set, the fact that he doesn't like people and created a business from it. He had a bunch of debt at that time and wanted to get his debt cleared as the motivation behind the sale. That led to us purchasing his online business. It was a great opportunity for us and I'm glad that we took the deal. It was a good synergy for our other business, Gemini Builds It, because it provided a whole other channel for transactions and the process was seamless.

After the deal with the online business was official, the prior businessman called me back and wanted to once again sell me the business that fell through. I want you to know that this was four years later and, due to problems he had with the company, the business was one-third the original size. He went on to tell me that he had left finance and was back working as a framing distributor. I called bullshit, because nobody retires from finance to go into framing, but I let him talk and to be honest, I can't remember what he was saying, all I remember is the fact that the market had changed, and I did not want his business.

Because he was so emotionally attached to the business, he did not want to sell it for the purchase price I offered back when we were negotiating. His refusal to compromise on the price created a situation, where four years later, he ended up having to liquidate his business. The moral of this story is that my best deal was the deal that I did not do.

We must pay attention to our gut with business decisions. It's like being back in high school and you have this major crush on someone where you can't think of anyone else. Then when you get the opportunity to be around them, you learn that they are not so good. When you want something so bad, there is usually something wrong with it.

The purchase of my online business was relatively seamless. We were both satisfied. The acquisition process went smoothly and that was a plus because when selling a business, both parties end up seeing each other past the day of closing. If a person is a jerk during the acquisition process, buyer beware. There are reps, warranties and things that linger on. There might also be more legal transactions that happen.

You do not want to be so emotional that whatever you chase runs away from you. Don't be so focused on one thing that causes you to make a bad buy. You have to know who you are dealing with. Make sure that you are doing deals with people who are more successful than you. Wealthier people have more to risk and more to lose than you do. Those are the people you want to deal with.

I try to avoid people who nickel and dime and have a scarcity mindset. Those people often are not enjoyable people. I find that it is so transferable, not just with business but with life in general. People who make a habit out of nickel and diming everyone will most likely try to do it in business.

My entire mindset is about reframing every day. If something bad happened the day prior, I reframe and say to myself, great, that was a good lesson. If it were good, I would think how lucky I am and look at all my opportunities. I show gratitude.

As you go on with your business journey, do not be so focused on making a deal happen that you act based off emotions. Understand that sometimes in your life, the best deals you do are the deals that you did not do. Be grateful in either situation. Remember there is no such thing as failure, only learning opportunities.

Takeaways

- Is there a time when you wanted to make a business deal that did not go through?
- How do you feel about that situation? Do you place such a big emphasis on failure? What happens if you fail?
- Do you feel that the deal not working out helped you in the long run?

Chapter 9

Hiring the Best People

"Know what you bring. Know what you don't bring. And build a team that covers everything you need."

Angie Hicks, founder of Angie's List

Hiring the best people is not just about finding individuals with the right skills. It is about finding people who align with your companies' values, culture and vision. Good employees can impact your business in a positive way and increase overall morale. It is extremely important to me that I have positive people at my company who have an excellent work ethic. We produce quality work and I know that good employees are more likely to produce good quality.

I have an HR partner named Susan Bondy who has worked with me since I was working at my corporate job. She is an amazing person who always sees the best in people and is one of the most optimistic people I know. She has been such an asset by helping me with my creativity and putting pieces together.

Working in a custom business, it is harder to train employees because the work we do is not common. None of the calls that we receive are the same and there are many things that employees need to be able to catch on the phone. Almost all the hiring that we do comes from referrals from other employees.

Employee satisfaction and retention is important. We offer referral bonuses and incentives to refer others to work for the company, which is something that can't be done if working for a massive company like Amazon. This saves us a lot of money because it is expensive and hard to hire and train people. You have to think of ways to make your team part of the solution.

Susan has been great at showing me that interactions with my employees cannot be transactional. When I started working right out of high school, I had a false sense of reality. I quickly learned that the real life does not work like the imaginary town of "Mayberry." Back to what I said in a previous chapter as a CEO and an owner of a company, everything that my employees go through trickles down and essentially becomes my problem. Whether it is someone going through a divorce, having maxed out credit cards and doesn't have enough money for gas, all their problems affect their work and become a problem of mine.

We had a twenty-five-year-old employee who had never seen his mother or father get up and go to work. Growing up he only saw two professions: drug dealer or prostitute. He had many children, came from poverty and wanted to break the cycle. He did just that by working his way up to a managerial position. He was a good man and a hard worker, when he started to experience major problems in his life he would look to Larry, my husband, for guidance and direction.

One time he called my husband at four o'clock in the morning crying because of an issue he was going through. It was then that I realized that many of my employees see my husband and I as part of their families. Those are the types of people that, as CEOs and leaders, we have to help make successful. In working to make our lives one percent better each day, we should also strive to make our employees' lives one percent better. That's the job of an entrepreneur, to lead everyone to a better place and future.

Susan and I would often say to each other that we have this company and are changing our lives and that is bigger than any sales we could make. It is not about my paycheck but my purpose, which is to change lives. The ages of my employees and those we hire is not as significant a factor as it used to be.

There was a shipping clerk who worked for us who was eight-five years old when I bought the company. He is an army vet and an extremely hard worker. He always showed up to work on time and never complained. Working made him happy and gave him purpose and he is someone who does not want to retire. He was able to continue working for our company as long as he was able to perform his job safely.

We do not discriminate based on his age. I find it beneficial to have a work culture where there is a range in the age of employees. The older employees can provide wisdom to the younger ones and the younger employees can assist older employees with new advancements in technology.

When you treat your employees right, they will treat your business right. How we measure employee satisfaction is by engagement. We look to see if employees are doing more or less than what their job description dictates. We look to see if employees are talking about their jobs positively outside of work. If they have the ability to advance in their position it ignites fire in their spirits.

As my husband and I started gaining success, we Continued focusing on how to give back to employees and make their lives richer. Eventually people get to a point in life where there is no longer a money grab but a purpose grab.

As CEOs and owners, we must appeal to our employees and validate them and their presence. The good news is that as entrepreneurs we can structure our businesses differently than big corporations, particularly in the hiring process. Keep this in mind and use it to your advantage in your business.

The people you hire can make or break your business. They play that big of a role in your success. Make sure that you hire the best people. Use your current employees to bring in applicants. Remember your company's reputation is on the line, and your employees represent you. Choose wisely.

Takeaways

- Have you ever worked with a coworker or employee that constantly got under your skin?
- What characteristics are important to you that you would like your employees and coworkers to possess?
- How do you hire as a tool to promote your business?

Chapter 10

Single Best Decision of My Life

"Sometimes, it's the smallest decisions that can change your life forever."

Keri Russell

PerFast is the name of our holding company. It stands for Larry Wright (the Perfect one) and Courtney Wright (the Fast One). My husband who is perfect in all things finance and operations, and myself, Courtney Wright, who is the starter and the pacesetter. The single best decision of my life was marrying Larry Wright and the second was bringing him into a day-to-day role in the company. I actually met my husband while working because he was one of our suppliers back in our younger days. He turned up at my workplace because I worked like an animal every day and had no free time. If I had waited until I could come up for air later in my thirties, I may have never found Larry or gotten married.

Years later, after we had been married, were raising our two children and enjoyed our time together, the time came to hire a CFO at my first company. At first, I was completely against the idea of having Larry at the company because, in my mind, I did not want to ruin my marriage. You hear all these horror stories about spouses who start working together and end up not tolerating each other and the marriage falls apart. To think about it now, I realize I possibly had imposter syndrome and did not want him to get on board with the company out of fear of being exposed to weaknesses.

Gary Arakelian, from my Vistage company, thought Larry would be a good idea because even though I was good at sales, my husband was good at business. He told me how good I was at selling and my husband is good at handling numbers and doing operations. He is incredibly detailed, and Gary felt that I could sell more if I let my husband handle those aspects. He is everything that I am not in terms of planning and forecasting. He handles the banks and I get to focus on my genius. Overall, the situation is a **win-win.**

In retrospect, it ended up being the best thing for the business and I almost ruined it out of fear. I was seeing a therapist at that time, and she raised an interesting question that I had to ask myself. When I resisted the idea of my husband working for the company, was it a valid concern or just fear? I have to pay attention when I react to something too quickly.

My husband and I have noncompeting skills that complement the company. We get to spend some of our days together and at times ride to work together. We are aligned with where our family is going. Some days are long, but overall, we are growing together. He operates 100 percent from logic and is grounded. When I am running off my nerves, his calmness comforts me and brings me back to earth. We can share our wins with each other and, when we make deals and major moves, are able to high-five each other at the end of the day.

Larry and I must continue to grow together and learn along the way. I absolutely have no regrets. **Best business decision ever.**

Takeaways

- Have you ever made a decision that impacted your life in a major way?
- In what ways and in which circumstances have you allowed fear to stop you from making a decision?
- Was the fear justified?

Chapter 11

Proximity is Power

"Surround yourself with only people who are going to lift you higher."

Oprah Winfrey

When I first started CDW merchants, it was two lieutenants and myself. The two lieutenants were a super talented sales guy that I worked with at my previous job and my sister. They both bet on me when I dragged them along as I started the company under the guise that my company was going to the moon. At that time, my company had twelve employees. Both the sales guy and my sister's earnings significantly increased after coming to work there. Even though their earnings increased, it was no cake walk as the business grew. Sometimes it seemed like we were making shit up with dust and mirrors. My business appeared to be greater than the actual size of the company at that time.

When I made the decision to sell my business, I did not tell anyone (this was a shareholder decision) and something I thought about long and hard. It was the right decision for my family and me at the time, but the risk was enormous. The inventory carrying cost was high, the cash flow was seasonal, and the headwinds for retail stores were strong.

It was surprising to me how the two VPs had such different reactions. One was thrilled at the prospect of moving up to a larger company with more opportunity and the other didn't want any part of it. I believe that what played into it was the un-said. Most people think of lots of things they want, perhaps feel they deserve and even expect, only most times I find they fail to communicate them.

The reason I have gotten so much out of business and life is because I asked for it. That situation showed me that most people don't ask for the things they want in life, and they should. I never understood why people can't bring forward the things they want. Is it because they think they will hurt someone's feelings? The worst thing that you can hear is no. You need to put your game face on and ask for what you want. No one is going to give you anything, if you want something you have to go and get it. You can't be afraid to ask for what you want, and you must know the right way to ask. Plain and simple is always the best approach.

The sales guy that worked for me was named Charles and he had a great attitude about the entire situation from the start. He came to me, telling me that he wanted to be a part of the company and had a desire to become a partner one day. Even though I admired his drive, I was honest with him and told him that this was not the right place for him if becoming a partner was his goal. I had to let him know that if his desire was to earn more than his friends, then he could make it happen. After our conversation, he told me he understood what I was saying, but he just had to ask about becoming a partner. I respected him for knowing what he wanted and not being afraid to ask.

One time, I went to my boss and asked for more money, and he gave me phantom shock. I found a way to solve my need because I asked. People should understand that when someone asks a question, it is not the end of the conversation, but the start of the conversation. I respect it when someone comes to me and asks for what they want.

Know what you want before you determine how to get there and who to be around. Vision boards are becoming increasingly popular with millennials and entrepreneurs as tools to help people obtain their goals and dreams. A vision board is something you create by getting a poster board and adding pictures of what it is you would like to accomplish or attain. When creating a vision board, you want to make it as detailed as possible. It should be people based, meaning you will also add the people that you want to have with you once you accomplish your goal. The vision board should invoke and be emotion filled. I am a believer in the power of creating vision boards.

Forbes details a survey completed by TD Bank that explored entrepreneurs and vision boards. The article, *"Survey Shows Visualizing Success Works*," written by Eilene Zimmerman, describes the outcome of vision boards. The survey was conducted on 11,000 individuals (about the seating capacity of Cameron basketball stadium at Duke University) and five hundred small business owners. Those who just imagined financial success and attaining their business goals felt confident that they would achieve them. Those who not only used their imagination, but also used visuals, were almost twice as confident.

Of the 20% of small business owners who used vision boards, 76% of those owners reported that their business was where they envisioned it would be when they started. 82% of small business owners who used vision boards from the start of their business reported that they had accomplished more than half of the goals they originally set for themselves.

99% of people go about the day thinking life will give them what they want, and the 1% of us do not accept that and say that we will get what we want and make it happen.

CDW merchants was named after me and my tagline was, “bringing your vision to life.” I trademarked that and I brought my vision to life. We had a broad vision, and I added the details. We had these broad strokes, and I painted a portrait. When I went out to my clients, they would give me adjectives and I created the picture. A client would say he wanted a pink holiday and sequins and I translated that into a 10-foot-tall pink tree that is all blinged out in sparkly, silver icing. Not only that, but I'm also getting the specific shade of pink, the type of sparkles, everything customized to the studs.

Sometimes people will ask me how I became so assertive and most times it makes me laugh because as a child, I was very shy. That shyness went out the window when I was fourteen years old and went to France. That was the most untethered I had ever been. My father was not there to speak for me, and I had to “work that muscle” and figure it out. I soon began to realize that good things started happening when I started to speak up for myself. That set me on the path of being fearless.

You are the average of the top five people you hang around with. I was the kid who never drank, never smoked, never did anything crazy (until college) and I try to teach this to my children. After getting sober at 21 years old and being sober since, I wasn't in the bars drinking when I was in my twenties like everyone else. I spent my time around educated people who were self-employed and those who were hard workers. That is what I became. People think that I am lucky, but is it that I am lucky, or did I make my own luck? The thought of being at home on Saturday nights at the age of twenty-two years old is not appealing to most.

I made my luck. The small amount of self-improvement I made each day with compound interest allowed me to create the life I have. It's like the sand in the hourglass. I am notorious for setting SMART goals for myself and my business. SMART goals are goals that are Specific, Measurable, Attainable, Realistic and have a Timeframe.

An article published by Michigan State University, "Achieving your Goals: An Evidence-Based Approach," discussed a study conducted by Psychology professor, Dr. Gail Matthews, over goal setting. In the study, participants were put into groups to determine the impact of setting SMART goals.

In one group, participants did not write their goals down. A second group set goals and wrote the goals down. A third group had the participants write down their goals and an action plan to commit. A fourth group wrote down goals, action plans to commit and provided the list to a friend. The last group of participants set goals, wrote them down along with commitment action plans, provided the list to a friend along with weekly updates.

The findings showed that 76% of participants who wrote down their goals, actions, provided it to a friend and provided weekly updates were successful at achieving them. This was 33% higher than those who did not write down their goals. The success rate of those who did not write them down was 43% achieved. SMART goals are beneficial to anyone who is serious about reaching certain accomplishments in their lives. Never underestimate the power of writing things down.

Being close to or in close connection with influential or successful people can lead to personal and professional growth. It can also lead to increased opportunities for advancement. I suggest that you pay close attention to the company that you keep and seek those who can benefit you. Never be afraid to network, attend seminars or join groups if it can help you professionally. You have the power to control your surroundings.

Takeaways

- Are there any ways that you can position yourself in proximity to those who you consider powerful?
- What types of people would you like to work with and do business with?
- Do you believe in the Power of Proximity?
- In what ways can you get into circles that will benefit you in the long run?

Chapter 12

Lady Boss

"Don't call me lucky. Call me a badass."

Shonda Rhimes

Although I have made many advancements in my professional career and business, to say that I did not face obstacles would be a lie. In my life, I have only worked for two jobs other than owning my businesses. Before becoming a business owner, many times I was the only woman in my department. For me to be a woman working amongst successful and powerful men, I always had to outwork all of them. Many of the men that I worked with also were not happy that I was their peer. I didn't care however, because I had found my path.

When I went to the Public Company in 2012, I was one of two general managers in North America. The company brought in four billion dollars in sales. My second year working for the company I was honored to win the "Manager of the Year" award. I got up on stage to accept my award and they put this large green, master's blazer on me, which was a man's coat as my "trophy". Clearly, they never considered what to do if a woman wins the award.

Although grateful, that annoyed me. I went to the bathroom and there was a woman inside who was crying. Once she saw me walk in, she wiped her face and explained to me that she has worked for the company for twenty years and has never seen a woman on that stage. I knew that I could not stay at that company. The culture was too male dominated and from what I heard; it may be a long time before real change is made.

Many major corporations are boy's clubs and not leveling. I always had to fight for my income, had to badger my way onto a level playing field and was tired of negotiating just for fair treatment.

The lady in the bathroom made me realize how some people see me as an inspiration. It is fulfilling for me when I help other women succeed. The desire to continue inspiring women and to get away from the boy's club is what led me to becoming an entrepreneur. I wanted to be a better mother. Being an entrepreneur allows me the ability to create the life that I want. The flexibility of entrepreneurship allows me to be present in my children's lives and it gave me my freedom.

Women have an advantage in business and leadership due to our emotional intelligence. What I have learned is that your EQ (emotional intelligence quotient) is more important than your IQ (intelligence quotient). IQ is so overrated. If you can read people, you can manage them. You gain wealth from compounding relationships. Work on your EQ muscle. A Harvard researcher composed a list of twelve traits that emotionally intelligent people possess that was published on CNBC.

Those 12 traits are:

- **Emotional self-awareness:** This is the ability to understand your own strengths and weaknesses.
- **Emotional self-control:** This is the ability to remain calm under pressure and the ability to recover quickly from anything that upsets you.
- **Adaptability:** This is the ability to be flexible and maintain agility when faced with change and uncertainty.
- **Achievement Orientation:** The ability to strive for and exceed a standard of excellence.
- **Positive outlook:** This is the ability to see the good in people, events and situations.

- **Empathy:** The ability to give full attention to another and attempt to understand what they are saying and how they are feeling.
- **Organizational awareness:** This is the ability to read emotional currents and dynamics within a group or business.
- **Influence:** This is the ability to be a natural leader who can gather support from others with ease.
- **Coach and Mentor:** This is the ability to foster learning through feedback and support.
- **Conflict management:** This is the ability to be comfortable dealing with disagreements between opposing sides and bring disputes out in the open to settle.
- **Teamwork:** The ability to interact good as a team member and working with others.
- **Inspirational Leadership:** The ability to guide and inspire others towards the company's overall vision.

In my younger days, I witnessed sellers that were always closing. They were loud and aggressive, and I felt like I needed to emulate them. Then I learned that I was different, and I started to lead with my heart, using EQ to further my career and business. You must own your own identity. You can't just copy others because what worked for them may not work for you. You must learn how to embrace your authentic self. People will become magnetized to you and softer in their approach.

It took a long time for me to see that most people do not think the way that I do. I tried to put myself in others' shoes and I must admit, it was hard at first. If you feel like you are different, own it, embrace it and appreciate it. It can be a lonely journey at times but find people that are like you. Many people will not relate to you and that is okay, stay on your path.

My current routine involves me waking up around 4:00 a.m. daily, seven days a week. I work out first thing in the morning and work out on most days. On the days that I do not work out, I take an hour to move around slowly. I try not to talk to anyone and take time to connect with myself. For me to wake up rested every morning, I must go to bed early. On most nights, I am in bed by 8:45 p.m. I do not give up any sleep and protect my sleeping pattern like a religion. It is that serious.

To have a clear mind, working out and getting adequate sleep is essential. It makes your job easier. I also make it a habit to read and work on personal development. Success and personal development go hand in hand and if you want to be successful, it won't happen without putting in the work to expand your knowledge. The books that I recommend reading are: *The Book of Why,* by Simon Simek. This book expanded my success and now I measure my success on a much broader scale. *Love Speaks,* by Sally Lou, is a book that showed me vulnerability.

In my *"Lady Boss with Courtney Wright"* podcast, we discuss all issues related to women in business that include marketing, customer experiences, building a brand, being a CEO and more. Women come on and share their stories and advice to empower other business owners. It is an amazing opportunity to share what we know.

For all my fellow "Lady Bosses," I salute you on your journey. Know that you are an inspiration to other women even if you do not realize it. Stay true to your vision, stay resilient and, if met with resistance, get creative and keep trying. Rome wasn't built in a day, and neither can your full success. The process can't be rushed, so try to enjoy the ride while you can and continue pursuing your dream.

Takeaways

- Do you embrace your true authentic self?
- What is currently stopping you from becoming the "Lady Boss" you know you were meant to be?
- How can you work on improving yourself and your business?

Conclusion

"I never dreamed about success. I worked for it."

Estee Lauder, Businesswoman

In conclusion, my journey to becoming a Lady Boss has been filled with knowledge, life-changing experiences, great relationships and lots of love for what I do (and HARD work). I shared some of my most memorable moments along the way that shaped how I do business and perform as a leader. I want it to serve you as a reminder that leadership knows no gender, and the world is hungry for the guidance, compassion, intelligence, drive and perspectives that only women bring to the table.

I've mentioned several times in this book how my dad and mom would tell me that I could be anything I wanted when I got older and how, in my early twenties, I thought that was a crock of bull. After reflecting on my business journey, I see that it was not bull and my father was right. I became exactly who I wanted to become. However, I would like to add to my father's statement and say that, yes, I could do it, but it does not come easy. I think that is a more accurate statement.

So now I say that to you. You can go out, pursue your passion and achieve your dreams if you are willing to put in the work.

To whom much is given, much is required. A true boss's job is never done, and you must know that nothing will be handed to you. Regardless, that is okay because I know you have the strength and guts to go out there and take it. All my accomplishments, as difficult they may have been, have been worth it. Currently I am the owner of Gemini Builds It, Showcase Acrylics and E commerce company, PerFast Holding and a podcast.

To think all of this came from me writing my one-page business plan and making up my mind that I was going to become my own boss. I know that I am walking in my purpose and continue to make it a mission of mine to help as many women as I can. My mother's advice to make my family a priority continues to resonate in my life. All my personal and professional decisions are made based on the well-being of my husband and children.

After you close this book remember that within you lies the power to lead others, inspire others and create change. Make sure that you find your genius, embrace your authenticity and set yourself apart from others. Let your voice be heard and know that you are not alone but are a part of a global sisterhood of women breaking barriers and redefining what is possible for them despite what someone else may have believed. That leadership role or business that you are working towards is more than an aspiration, it is your calling and destiny. Don't be afraid to answer the call.

What vision are you ready to make come to life?

Made in the USA
Monee, IL
02 February 2024

52790164R00066